(Page 1) Soldiers direct artillery from a "fire-direction center" in an armored vehicle. (Pages 2-3) Tackling the final barrier in an obstacle course, soldiers train for the Special Forces. (Pages 4-5) Camouflaged soldiers patrol in the murky twilight. The silhouette of a short-whip antenna reveals the soldier at far right to be the squad's radio telephone operator. (Pages 6-7) An infantry squad disembarks from the rear of an M-2 Bradley armored personnel carrier. (Pages 8-9) Paratroopers from the 82nd Airborne Division land during a mass tactical exercise over a North Carolina drop zone. (Pages 10-11) Two AH-64 Apaches on the prowl. (Page 12) A soldier relaxes after a mission. (Page 14) A soldier of the elite 3d Infantry "Old Guard," which provides hand-picked guards for the most sensitive national localities in the Washington, D.C., area, including the Tomb of the Unknown Soldier.

Color Photo Credits: **Robert Bruce/IDI** photos appear on pages 76, 77, 81 (bottom), 132, 134, 135, and 205. **Rick Diaz/IDI** photo appears on page 160. **Hans Halberstadt** photos appear on pages 2-3, 12, 66, 96-97, 98, 99, 102, 103, 109, 136, 137, 144, 145, 158-159, 162, 173, 178, 182, 183, 194, 206-207, and 208. **David Hathcox/IDI** photos appear on pages 164, 165, and 172. **Gary L. Keiffer/IDI** photos appear on pages 83, 90, 92-93, 114-115, 116, 117, 122, 123, 166-167, 170-171, 174, 177, 179, and front dust jacket. **Mi Seitelman/IDI** photos appear on pages 72, 73, 78, 84-85, 86, 89, 94, 95, 101, 138, 139, 152, 156, 157, 163, 175, 176, 180, 197, and 198. **Fred Sutter** photos appear on pages 6-7, 10-11, 14, 56-57, 60, 61, 63, 67, 71, 74-75, 88, 120, 121, 125, 127, 128-129, 130, 131, 140, 146-147, 151, 153, 190, 191, 195, 196, 199, 202-203 and 204. **U.S. Army** photos appear courtesy of the U.S. Government, as represented by the Secretary of the Army, on pages 1, 4-5, 8-9, 58, 64, 65, 68, 69, 70, 79, 80, 81 (top), 82, 87 (top and bottom), 91, 100, 104-105, 106, 107, 108, 110, 111, 112, 113, 118-119, 124, 126, 133, 141, 142, 143, 148, 149, 150, 154-155, 161, 168, 169, 181, 184-185, 186, 187, 188, 189, 192, 193, 200, 201, and back dust jacket.

Archival Photo Credits: Photos on pages 20-38 and 40-43 appear courtesy of the National Archives; those on pages 39, 44-46, 49-51, and 54-55 appear courtesy of the U.S. Army; that on page 47 appears courtesy of PACIFIC STARS AND STRIPES; and those on pages 49 and 52-53 appear courtesy of the Army News Feature.

The publishers extends a special thanks to Lieutenant Colonel William Randall, whose patience stood the test of numerous questions and whose answers helped in the preparation of this book.

Designed by Carolyn Weary. Edited by Kathleen D. Valenzi. Design assistance provided by Natalie Hamilton. Color photo research conducted by Jonathan Scott Arms. Text written by Shelby L. Stanton and Teresa Riordan. Introduction and "The Solder's Mission" copyright © 1990 Shelby L. Stanton. All rights reserved. Remaining text copyright © 1990 Howell Press, Inc. All rights reserved. Hans Halberstadt photos copyright © 1990 Hans Halberstadt. All rights reserved. Fred Sutter photos copyright © 1990 Fred Sutter. All rights reserved. All other color photos, except those provided by the U.S. Army and those previously indicated, copyright © 1990 International Defense Images. All rights reserved. This book, or any portions thereof, may not be reproduced or transmitted in any form or by any means, electronic or mechanical, including photocopying, recording, or by any information storage and retrieval system, without permission in writing from the publisher. Library of Congress Catalog Card Number 89-80795. ISBN 0-943231-22-1. Printed and bound in Japan by Dai Nippon Printing Co., Ltd. Published by Howell Press, Inc., 700 Harris Street, Suite B, Charlottesville, VA 22901. Telephone (804) 977-4006. First printing.

HOWELL PRESS

SOLDIERS

A PORTRAIT OF THE UNITED STATES ARMY

TEXT BY SHELBY L. STANTON

VANGUARDS OF DEMOCRACY

Soldiering is part of the American character, and the accomplishments of soldiers serve as the foundation for our nation's greatness. The first European settlers doubled as soldiers in a hostile wilderness. Minutemen and other patriot soldiers forged the nation's independence. Expeditions composed of Army soldiers explored, mapped, and recorded the geography of a vast continent. Coast artillery soldiers manned harbor defenses that discouraged foreign invasion. Blue-garbed soldiers purged society of slavery and prevented the nation from being torn asunder by rebellion. The westward expansion was shielded by horse- and rail-mobile foot soldiers, often acting in concert with Native American scouting soldiers. Within our own century, soldiers have protected American interests and citizens from Peking to Panama, liberated countless millions of global inhabitants from tyranny and poverty, and fought to preserve American allies and democratic ideals throughout the world.

The United States Army boasts a history of more than 200-years' service and exists today as one of the world's oldest military organizations. One currently serving Massachusetts National Guard military police company was first organized in 1639 at Plymouth Colony, and selected elements from Puerto Rico and Florida date their heritage to the earliest Spanish settlements in the New World. This is the Army, however, of history books.

During my youth, the real Army was represented by legions of returning World War II soldier-citizens who were now our fathers, neighbors, and town officials. Their decorated uniform jackets hung in virtually every closet. The actual battle gear, from green steel-pot helmets to khaki ammunition belts, could be purchased for pocket change at the local surplus store. Movies and television recounted the stories they were too modest to tell: the beach assaults, the parachute drops, the battles through hedgerow and jungle, the clash of tanks in the Belgian snow. Our classroom wall maps rolled down to reveal the mechanics of their great triumph—multiple blue arrows snaking out of North America and slashing through broken red lines in both directions.

The World War II Army was the greatest land force ever fielded by the United States. We anticipated the day when we would shoulder arms in the tradition of our elders. As we grew older, however, we heard that the rules of warfare had changed. The days of sniping and bayonet charges were supposedly over. The meager efforts of individual soldiers would be overwhelmed by brilliant fireballs of multiple nuclear exchanges in future conflicts. Army units were scattered as faithful sentinels in hundreds of overseas locations, but their actual utility in case of hostilities was disputed.

As the years passed a new brand of warfare developed that placed the Army back in the forefront of active-duty considerations. An alarming number of insurgent and guerilla movements threatened American allies throughout Asia, South America, and Africa. At the same time, there was a sharp increase in militant confrontations between the superpowers and growing internal civil unrest.

Television contained fewer programs about the "big war." Instead, the screen featured nightly news reports showing the Army in a far different role. Gloved soldiers in crisp fatigues and chin-strapped helmets were manning checkpoints along the Berlin Wall, readying for deployment against Cuba, rescuing hostages in the Congo, and even guarding minority students on high school campuses. Then a new wave of urgent crises flashed across the screen with the exotic ring of distant tropics: Indonesia, Laos, Cambodia, Vietnam.

I completed my first training as a soldier at Fort Polk, Louisiana, during the height of the Vietnam war. At that time no troop unit was garrisoned at the post; it was simply a training mill. We marched, practiced quick-fire techniques, and trained on barren rifle ranges and marshy swamp thickets in either the blazing heat or pouring rain. We sweated through humid nights in double-tiered bunks lining the walls of antiquated wooden barracks or huddled miserably underneath field shelter halves during nocturnal thunderstorms. The accelerated soldier training at Polk was completely combat oriented. The next stop for most of us was the Vietnam battlefield.

Our sergeants wore fatigues with brightly colored shoulder patches and white name tapes and donned olive-green baseball caps marred by wiggle salt lines. The line sergeants of this Army learned how to soldier while climbing and fighting across the steep ridges of Korea. Their combat lessons were gleaned from places like the Bowling Alley or Heartbreak Ridge. During the day we practiced airmobile tactics on helicopters and cleared mock Viet Cong villages. During the evenings we listened as our sergeants recalled the decisive bark of Browning Automatic Rifles breaking up Chinese grenadier assaults against snowy boulder-strewn strongpoints, until the starry Louisiana skies seemed to ring with the shrill blast of enemy bugles.

By the time I reached Fort Bragg, North Carolina, a year later, the drill sergeants were wearing Smokey Bear hats, and their colorful patches had been replaced by subdued olive-drab insignia. Gleaming officer rank badges and noncommissioned officer chevrons were supplanted by black pin-on collar miniatures. The war in Vietnam was in its latter stages, but the long shadow of that conflict had clearly darkened the uniforms, the very essence of a soldier's identification.

Within the military, uniform alterations mark the passage of eras, just as geological time is branded in zones of rock along a mountain wall. The older hands reminded us of the brown-shoe army that preceded our black boots. Now we could reminisce about the stable training conditions and high prewar quality of the former white name-tape army.

The difference in the Army was profound. The number of Korean veteran noncommissioned officers in our ranks was dwindling rapidly. They were either leaving the service, serving second and third tours in Vietnam as senior advisors, or becoming casualties of the latest conflict. Except for a few shake-and-bake graduates fresh out of NCO schools, most of our younger junior sergeants had earned their stripes leading troops in close combat across the broken rice paddies and triple-canopy jungles of Vietnam. Our regular soldiers were disenchanted with the seemingly unfathomable war in Southeast Asia and tired of the "Mickey Mouse" police calls, kitchen duties, and guard-post assignments that typified stateside service.

My own personal quest for the old style of soldiering took me through both parachutist and ranger courses and, finally, to the Special Forces school. Upon donning the Green Beret, I caught up again with the imagined Army of my youth: a fighting group of spirited professionals who were committed to destroying the enemy on its own ground. We blazed trails across borders and pushed deep into remote enemy sanctuaries, but we paid a high price for our achievements. Individually, we lost many comrades in sudden fire fights or forlorn ambuscades. Many of us were invalided out of the service after being wounded in action, and others suffered career setbacks in an Army intolerant of unconventional methods. Collectively, our nation's special warfare capability was virtually destroyed.

When I departed the armed forces as a captain, the Army was entering its hardest transition within a century. For the first time since before World War II, the Army was terminating its dependence on the draft as a source of enlistment and was converting to an all-volunteer component. Following a difficult period of adjustment, the Army was rebuilt as one of the finest in our nation's history. This success resulted from the soldiering dedication of those officers and sergeants who insured that the continuity of Army tradition was passed to a new generation of soldiers.

Today's Kevlar-helmeted Army represents a far different military force than the "steel pot" Army we grew up studying in school, hearing about in Korea, and serving with in Vietnam. The units are more specialized and the soldiers are more sophisticated. The termination of the draft ended the wild fluctuations in soldier quality that mixed graduate scholars with category-four mental incompetents in the same squads. The modern Army soldiers are, on the average, brighter and more homogeneous, and this leveling of ability translates into easier management and skills-acquisition training. Unnecessary duties that sapped unit training time were also scrapped, including kitchen police and other detested housekeeping chores.

The physical conditioning of today's soldier emphasizes cardiovascular shape rather than the misleading results of the Vietnam-era Army's physical training test. The latter was a five-event course taken in full combat gear that included the grenade throw; the run, dodge, and jump; the low crawl; the monkey-bars; and the mile run. Supposedly geared to simulate actual soldier skills, its relatively undemanding nature enabled many physically unfit individuals to remain in service. Although the modern three-event test can be taken in a gym suit, the required sit-ups, push-ups, and two-mile run give a much better picture of a soldier's actual physical status. Combat-wise veterans, however, still remark that no soldier will run one or two miles in battle; a 25-meter dash would be more realistic.

In addition to improved soldier quality, the Army is far better prepared doctrinally to wage war. The improvised tactical reaction to combat that typified our Vietnam-era Army has been replaced by an AirLand Battle concept that anticipates the in-depth battlefield. The combat zone is now the main battle area, the lines of communication that bedeviled our logistical efforts are now accounted for as the rear battle area, and the rarely penetrated main enemy-base areas of our Asian experience are now properly targeted as the deep battle area. Whereas our Vietnam-based Army battalions maneuvered with only patched-in air assets, today's battalions are programmed in advance to fight in a joint environment with locked-in frontal aviation.

Today's "Total Army" is composed of a triad of fighting forces. These are the Regular Army, the Army Reserve, and the Army National Guard. This combination is kept in constant battle readiness with the finest training and latest equipment and is geared to provide the nation with an expanded, highly mobile military capability during national emergencies.

The Total Army concept is based on the realization that modern warfare demands instant battlefield response. In a world compressed by the need for rapid military maneuver, Army planners cannot depend on the comparatively leisurely mobilization experiences of previous conflicts. The Army is committed to a series of war plans that necessitate swift response on a global scale. The Total Army insures that all components meet the same high standards, even to

the extent of immediate pairing of selected Reserve and National Guard brigades with Regular Army divisions in case of war.

Today's Total Army represents a radical departure from the country's past military practices. Reserve and militia contingents have reinforced the Regular Army in every war, but they were usually separated by a wide gulf in standards of preparedness and fighting expectations. For most of their existence, state militias (now the National Guard) relied on local funding and were only as competent as their leaders and individual budgets permitted. Many National Guard elements acted more as social clubs than combat organizations and required extensive reorganization whenever called into national service. For decades Army Reserve units languished as poor relatives to their Active service counterparts, being saddled with obsolete equipment and inferior training opportunities.

By the time I joined the Army during the Vietnam conflict, political circumstances had reduced most National Guard and Army Reserve units to their lowest point of combat efficiency. Widespread popular sentiment against mass mobilization insured the continuing immunity of these forces from active service. For many, joining the National Guard became a convenient way of meeting their military obligation without incurring the risk of actual combat duty. The relatively safe haven offered by such units during time of war swelled their ranks, but it was an enforced volunteerism prompted by avoidance of the draft. In addition, the Regular Army stripped many Reserve units of vital equipment in order to supply our "fighting Army" and its allies with gear and weapons.

Some National Guard and Army Reserve units were mobilized during the course of the protracted Vietnam conflict, but they represented a minuscule fraction of those available. Only a few units were sent to Vietnam, but the Army faced great problems in making them combat-ready. These included a high rate of non-deployable people, extensive retraining, issuance of and familiarization with new weapons, and even litigation concerning the mobilization's legality.

The bitter experience underscored the value of making the postwar National Guard and Army Reserve an integral part of the Total Army team.

The Regular Army currently contains more than 760,000 soldiers organized into 18 divisions around the world. Most armor division soldiers are posted to Europe and serve in either the 1st Armored Division ("Old Ironsides"), the 3d Armored Division ("Spearhead"), or the forward brigade of the 2d Armored Division ("Hell on Wheels"). Other armor division soldiers are posted either to the remainder of the latter division or to the 1st Cavalry Division ("First Team") at Fort Hood, Texas. The cavalry division is a heavy armored formation that depends on the Mississippi Army National Guard 155th Armored Brigade for round-out purposes in case of mobilization.

Mechanized infantry division soldiers are stationed with the 1st Infantry Division ("Big Red One") at Fort Riley, Kansas; the 3d Infantry Division ("Marne Division") in Germany; the 4th Infantry Division ("Ivy Division") at Fort Carson, Colorado; the 5th Infantry Division ("Red Diamond") at Fort Polk, Louisiana; the 8th Infantry Division ("Pathfinder") in Germany; and the 24th Infantry Division ("Victory Division") at Fort Stewart, Georgia. Of these divisions, the 5th and 24th depend on round-out brigades from the Louisiana Army National Guard 256th and Georgia Army National Guard 48th Infantry Brigades, respectively, to reach full battle strength in time of war.

Light division soldiers serve with either the 6th Infantry Division at Fort Richardson, Alaska; the 7th Infantry Division ("Bayonet") at Fort Ord, California; the 10th Mountain Division at Fort Drum, New York; or the 25th Infantry Division ("Tropic Lightning") at Schofield Barracks, Hawaii. The Army Reserve 205th Infantry Brigade is programmed to round out the 6th Division, and the New York Army National Guard 27th Infantry Brigade has orders to join the 10th Mountain Division upon mobilization.

Other infantry division soldiers are assigned to either the 2d Infantry Division ("Indianhead")—a specialized, reinforced division guarding the Korean Demilitarized Zone—

or the 9th Infantry Division ("Old Reliables") at Fort Lewis, Washington—a prototype motorized division currently slated for conversion to either light or mechanized status. Parachutist division soldiers are assigned to the 82d Airborne Division ("All American") at Fort Bragg, North Carolina. Air assault division soldiers are assigned to the 101st Airborne Division ("Screaming Eagles") at Fort Campbell, Kentucky. Non-divisional soldiers are posted to the many separate brigades and other units within the Regular Army inventory.

The Army has also revitalized its special warfare capability to the point that the Special Forces is now recognized as a separate branch. Our modern Special Forces groups are well diversified in combating terrorists, assisting partisan movements, training indigenous forces, and conducting lightning raids against strategic targets. Today's Special Forces troopers are an integrated part of the Army machine and stand alongside the rangers as the cutting edge of our Army's skilled commando force.

Today's Army Reserve soldier is no longer an uncertain shadow to a Regular Army counterpart. Benefitting immensely from almost two decades of intense prewar personnel selection and rearming policies, the soldiers of the Army Reserve stand ready to meet their Congressional directives. These charge the Army Reserve with providing trained units and qualified soldiers for active duty in the armed forces, under any circumstances relating to the country's national security.

The Army Reserve is composed of four types of soldiers. About 300,000 reservists are part of the Individual Ready Reserve. These members have completed their active duty service, but still have a military obligation and are subject to recall in national emergency. They are not, however, part of any troop program unit. Another 228,000 reservists are part of reserve units and are paid to drill each weekend and complete a two-week exercise with their unit during the year. Approximately 14,000 reservists are Individual Mobilization Augmentees with assignments to specific positions in event of mobilization. Finally, about 13,000 members of the Active Reserve serve full-time duty administering Reserve programs.

The Army Reserve is structured both to fulfill its peacetime training role and to provide organized units in case of hostilities. The 21 administrative Army Reserve Commands will disappear in time of war, leaving 49 General Officer Commands to join the active armed forces as fully functional units. For example, in event of war the Army Reserve 205th Infantry Brigade is scheduled to report to its mobilization station in Minnesota and provide the additional brigade to round out the Regular Army 6th Infantry Division in Alaska.

The projected utilization of reserve units as combat-dependable, "on-call" elements to supplement Regular Army formations signifies the current importance of the Army Reserve in the national defense. To assure optimum performance levels, the Reserve expanded its overseas deployment training dramatically during the 1980s. By the end of the decade, over 1,000 reserve units participated in overseas training exercises from "Team Spirit" in Korea to "Northern Viking" in Iceland. Several exercises were conducted deliberately in troubled regions, including "Bright Star" in the Middle East and "Fuertes Caminos" in Central America. This realistic training, conducted alongside Regular Army units, has been invaluable in verifying actual reserve capabilities and limitations.

The third brace of the Total Army is the Army National Guard. This component has been part of the first-line defenses of the United States since 1775 and continues the traditional militia mission of assisting state authorities in times of civil disturbance or national calamity. The National Guard is the nation's only armed force having both federal and state responsibilities. This unique role involves National Guard soldiers in a wide spectrum of assignments, ranging from local drug enforcement to reinforcement of Regular Army divisions in case of war.

The Army National Guard has 455,000 soldiers and is presently at its highest recorded strength in history. This is a special tribute to the professionalism of its members, who are now true volunteers with no prompting of the draft behind their motivations. The Army National Guard training is intense and geared to Regular Army standards. During 1989, for example, National Guard soldiers trained in 45 different countries in a wide variety of assignments that often supplemented Regular Army operations.

The Army National Guard's roots in state militia service have provided it with a colorful array of unusual units. Among these are the three battalions of Eskimo Scouts within the 297th Infantry Brigade. The Eskimo Scouts' own 207th Infantry Brigade (a part of the brigade) is organized along the lines of a Special Forces group. These highly skilled warrior-scouts actively patrol the Alaskan shoreline and rugged interior in small teams alert to infiltration or signs of enemy activity. Another special National Guard outfit is composed of mountain soldiers in the 3d Battalion, 172d Infantry Regiment. The mountain battalion comprises ski-qualified, infantry-mountaineering companies from Maine, Vermont, New Hampshire, and New York.

The soldiers of the Total Army—whether in the Regular Army, Army Reserve, or Army National Guard—are interdependent for their wartime mission accomplishments. Regular Army soldiers are about evenly divided between combat and combat support units, but a mere three percent occupy combat service support roles within transportation, maintenance, supply, and medical organizations. At the same time, fully 60 percent of Army Reservists and 27 percent of soldiers serving in the National Guard are slotted in critical combat service support elements.

The Army soldier remains the prime guardian of our national security. The legacy of our soldiers is rooted in the very liberation of the nation and was instrumental in shaping its physical and moral dimensions. United States Army soldiers continue to serve honorably as a vanguard for democracy, and they serve with the knowledge that the fate of the free world still rests on their shoulders.

—Shelby Stanton

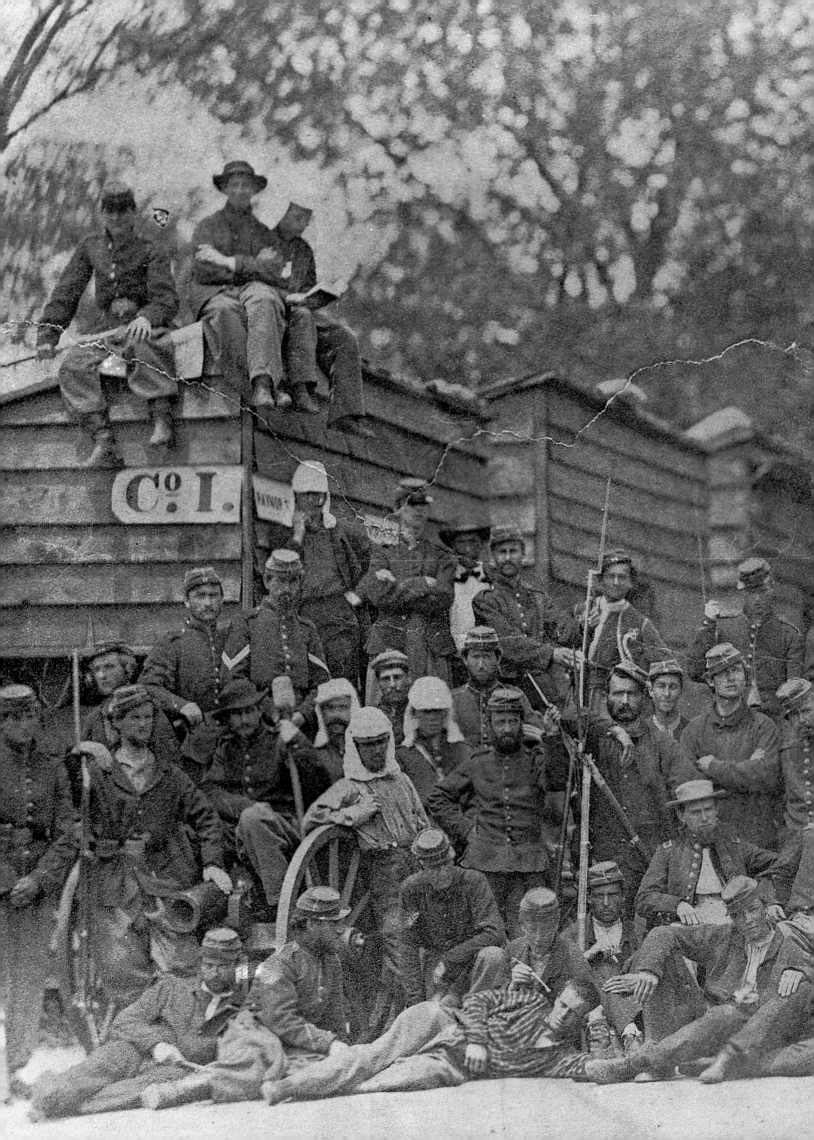

(Above) Seasoned veterans of the 4th Michigan—a battle-hardened regiment that fought past Gaine's Mill, Malvern Hill, and the Wheatfield at Gettysburg—prepare for action within the Wilderness of Virginia during the regiment's last campaign of the Civil War. (Overleaf, pages 20-21) Soldiers of the 12th New York Infantry relax between skirmishes. This unit was typical of limited-service state regiments that sustained heavy losses in early Civil War combat (in this case, at Blackburn's Ford, Virginia) but which retained enough volunteers who extended beyond their original term of enlistment to field a battalion late in the war.

Most Civil War soldiers were state volunteers of uneven quality who became capable professionals after a few weeks' active drilling and campaigning. These troops demonstrate their newly acquired military proficiency for the camera by forming a defensive square, while a contingent of cavalry looks on.

Army soldiers of the 9th Infantry assemble in Santiago Plaza as the Spanish surrender the besieged Cuban town on July 17, 1898. Santiago's negotiated capture avoided a costly battle for its possession, but the victorious troops were still subjected to the ravages of Yellow Fever.

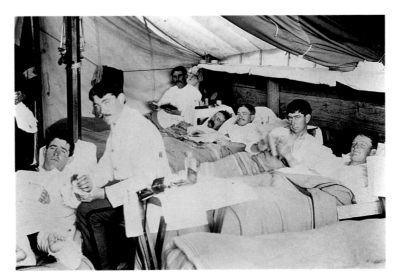

(Top) Patients of the 3d Cavalry at Camp McKenzie, Pennsylvania, were stricken by illness before they even embarked for the battlefront in Cuba. **(Center)** Nurses aboard a U.S. hospital ship located in Cuba's Siboney harbor maintained the overall good health of the U.S. expeditionary force. **(Bottom)** The Battle of San Juan Hill, one of the most notable engagements of the Spanish-American War, demonstrated the new solidarity between U.S. soldiers from the North and South. Here an ambulance retrieves casualties after the battle.

Regular Army officers of the 21st Infantry pose for the camera in the stifling tropical heat of Cuba. During the Spanish-American War, Army officers seldom had occasion to lead marching ranks of troops into battle, because the war was fought largely along jungle trails, "bomb-proofs," and trench lines.

Members of the 3d Cavalry ride with full colors in review formation during the Spanish-American War. These resplendent cavalrymen, however, fought primarily as ordinary dismounted soldiers at El Caney, San Juan Hill, Aquadores, and Santiago.

Army soldiers arriving from the United States march across London's Westminster Bridge on their way to board ships for the final stage of their voyage to France. The arrival of large numbers of U.S. troops on the front during 1917 insured the destruction of the German armed forces in the First World War.

(Above) Relaxing only briefly, Army soldiers take a short rest after capturing a German secondary trench line in the Argonne Forest, 1918. The Army's rapid advance during this stage of the war had taken these troops beyond the main front's barren wasteland and into the heavily vegetated woodland of former German rear areas. (Right) Armed with a French light machine gun, these Army soldiers hold a portion of the Vosages sector in 1918. Automatic weapons became a common, yet essential, part of the infantry arsenal during World War I. (Facing) Army signal corpsmen use a captured German field phone during the battle for the St. Mihiel salient in 1918. Improved wire communications provided the soldier with ready access to supporting weapons, especially artillery and machine guns, and greatly increased his combat effectiveness.

(Above) The U.S. Army soldier was often more fortunate than his allies in both living accommodations and intensity of sustained combat. These troops enjoy the relatively dry luxury of raised bunks in a shell-riddled, temporary "barracks" near Beauval, France, 1918. **(Facing)** Trench warfare was an integral part of a soldier's life during World War I. This Army artilleryman huddles near the entrance of his protective "shell splinter-proof" bunker along a trench line, and uses the open doorway to shine light on the letter he is writing home.

Lightly wounded soldiers returning by truck from the St. Mihiel front converse and joke with comrades behind the lines. The Army emphasized fire and movement in its battlefield maneuvering and avoided the frightful casualties incurred by other nations employing constant frontal attacks.

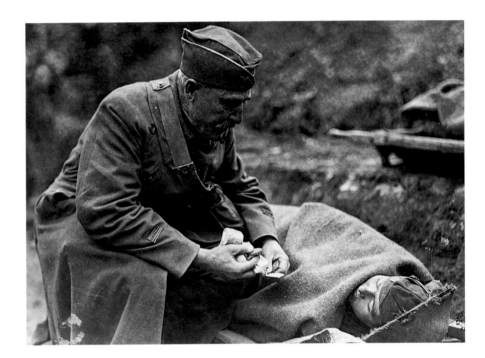

(Top) An American Red Cross field worker comforts a soldier wounded in the Argonne Forest fighting during 1918. WWI medical science was primitive by modern standards, but it was the first major war in which doctors understood the importance of preventing shock and infection among casualties. **(Bottom)** This ambulance, mired in a ditch after sliding on a rain-swept roadway, serves as mute testimony to the mishaps that sometimes accompanied motorization. The Army's motor vehicles of World War I had only limited power and traction, but they provided the U.S. military with a previously unknown degree of wartime transport flexibility. **(Overleaf, pages 36-37)** A caravan of jeeps passes between twin churches in Rome as Army soldiers advance through Italy during June 1944. The U.S. Army was committed to both defeating the enemy war machine and rebuilding liberated areas during its advance through Europe in World War II.

Army crewmen of an armored scout vehicle racing past shattered German positions in Normandy toward Brittany, France, pause briefly to pass out rations to elderly citizens during World War II. The generosity, compassion, and civic spirit of the U.S. Army soldier has remained constant in all wars.

Dismounted soldiers of the 14th Armored Division rush down a burning German street as they clear a pathway for tanks through Hoellrich on April 6, 1945. The foot soldier is necessary, even in mechanized warfare, to provide a vital shield against potential anti-tank positions that could devastate an armored column at close range.

Wading onto a hostile New Guinea beach from the gaping front ramp of a giant Landing Ship Tank (LST), these Army soldiers push the allied lines closer to the Philippines in World War II. Throughout the Pacific campaign, the Army worked in close conjunction with U.S. Navy assets to "leap-frog" past Japanese strongpoints.

Apprehensive, yet confident, these Army soldiers in a Coast Guard landing craft approach the beach during the 1944 invasion of Aitape, New Guinea. During the war, the Army trained many of its soldiers in specialized amphibious and airborne doctrine as well as standard infantry warfare.

The Guadalcanal campaign was the first example of standard Army-Marine maneuvering during World War II, wherein the Marines made the initial invasion and received Army reinforcing support. Such support was often programmed to eventually supplant the Marine presence, thus freeing the Marines for further amphibious assaults. Here reinforcing Army troops move through a tropical quagmire to reach the main battle line on Guadalcanal.

(Above) Army soldiers use a light mortar to pound suspected Japanese positions on Attu, in the Alaskan Aleutian Island chain, as part of the 1943 offensive that cleared enemy troops from American soil during World War II. Within that conflict, the Army soldier fought in all climates —from the tundra slopes of this icy battlefield to the desert sands of Saharan North Africa. **(Overleaf, pages 44-45)** Praying chaplains and busy medics attend the triage at a forward collecting point for soldiers wounded in heavy fighting along the Pusan perimeter in Korea, July 1950. Despite a lack of equipment and initial combat experience, these soldiers held the line against incessant enemy onslaughts in the first months of the Korean war.

Soldiers of the 7th Infantry Division march into battle after participating in General MacArthur's brilliant amphibious landing behind enemy lines at Inchon, Korea, in September 1950. By this stage of the war, the thin American ranks were reinforced by South Korean "Augmentation" troops—many of whom can be seen here—to bring field units up to fighting strength.

A soldier with a light anti-tank weapon slung over his back, dashes forward under fire to deliver suppressive fire against a Viet Cong bunker that has pinned his comrades close to the ground near Chu Lai, Vietnam, in 1968. Soldiers must often depend on their own portable weapons to gain a firepower advantage in close fighting.

(Above) Perched precariously on a cliffside ledge, a recoilless-rifleman of the 3rd Infantry "Bayonet" Division watches over a frozen plateau for Chinese troops approaching the final defensive lines at Hungnam during the allied evacuation of northern Korea. The courageous fortitude of the American soldier was amply demonstrated during this bitter winter campaign. **(Facing)** High above the tree tops, a long-range infantry patrol of the 173d Airborne Brigade rappels into a triple-canopy jungle of South Vietnam's central highlands to search out secret Viet Cong base areas. This helicopter-delivered flexibility, regardless of terrain obstacles, became a mainstay of soldiering in the Vietnam conflict.

A parachutist of the 173d Airborne Brigade crawls through underbrush to close within grenade-throwing distance of an enemy machine gun during a hillside firefight near Dak To, Vietnam, in 1967. Maneuvering low to the ground is perhaps the most timeless tactic for increasing the odds of a soldier's survival in crossing hostile territory.

Sky troopers of the 1st Cavalry Division (Airmobile) are airlifted by helicopter onto the battlefield during the crucial Ia Drang Valley campaign
in the highlands of Vietnam, October 1965. This important campaign
established helicopter airmobility as a staple of Army maneuverability
in modern warfare.

Silhouetted by a protective smoke screen, a machine gunner advances toward a North Vietnamese Army-occupied trench line near Tuy Hoa, Vietnam. He is followed by his assistant gunner carrying spare ammunition boxes. The machine gun serves as one of the soldier's most trusted and powerful weapons in combat.

(Above) The vanguard of a 27th Infantry "Wolfhounds" Battalion of the 25th Infantry Division "Tropic Lightning" crosses a marsh in the contested Plains of Reeds west of Hiep Hoa, Vietnam, during June 1969. The leading platoon officer is followed by an array of radio antennas carried by his radiomen, who provide the crucial link between the soldiers and their supporting aviation, artillery, and naval gunfire. (Facing) On the lookout for snipers and sudden ambush, troopers of the 101st Airborne Division move cautiously into a remote enemy jungle bastion in northern South Vietnam during 1971. The towels are carried to wipe off perspiration and pad shoulder-carried weapons; the rope coil is used to cross swift mountain streams.

TRAINING: THE BEDROCK OF THE ARMY

It was the summer of 1777 and General George Washington's forces had just suffered a series of humiliating defeats in the vicinity of Philadelphia. Washington decided to camp at Valley Forge and engage in some serious rebuilding for the Army. His command was deficient in just about everything—from supplies to organization and training. Troops deployed as 13 separate state military forces instead of as a unified force; and the soldiers were not standardized in either equipment or fighting techniques. Washington's biggest concern, however, was the Army's lack of training. In desperation he turned to Major General Friedrich W. A. Baron von Steuben, a German military expert who had volunteered his services to the Continentals. Under Washington's directive, Steuben became the Army's Inspector General; his mandate, to train the troops. Surveying his ragtag, ill-fed, ill-clothed men for the first time, Steuben complained, "In European armies a man who has drilled for three months is called a recruit; here in two months I must have a soldier."

Despite the "von" in his name, Steuben was not an aristocrat. Nor was the title "Major General" that he flaunted legitimate. He had indeed served in the Army of Frederick the Great, but it had been as an obscure captain. Steuben's exaggerations didn't matter, though, because he was a natural leader and good at training soldiers. The men of the Continental Army adored him, because Steuben respected them as genuine, uniquely American soldiers, rather than condescending to them as imitations of European troops.

Steuben undertook three fundamental reforms. First, he made officers responsible for training their men. This delegation of authority strengthened loyalty between the ranks of men while improving everyone's military skills. Second, he standardized formations and drills, replacing a variety of European army texts with a specifically "American" way of doing things. Third, and perhaps most crucial, he taught the Continental Army to march in columns of fours. Until Steuben arrived, many troops had a tendency to proceed to the battle front in a disheveled line.

Week two of the intense air assault training course of the 101st Airborne Division includes climbing a ladder obstacle that tests the endurance of the soldier.

Steuben also consolidated Continental regiments into standardized training battalions of 200 men each, making for an easier, faster, and more predictable deployment of troops to the front line.

To disseminate his reforms, Steuben served as drill sergeant to a model company of officers. After drilling them personally, he dispatched the officers to train the rest of the Army. He also put his training principles in writing. *Steuben's Regulations for the Order and Discipline of the Troops of the United States* laid out drill regulations, tactics, and general military routine. Better known as the "Blue Book," it remained the official American military manual for 33 years.

When Washington's Army broke camp the following spring, it was prepared to fight. The soldiers' newly acquired skills led them to victory, and a vital lesson was learned: in order for an army to succeed, it must be well trained. The importance of training is still recognized today.

Camouflaged tanks and armored troop carriers scurry across the eery, twilight moonscape of the Mojave Desert. Soldiers sprint to a ridge, preparing to attack. A radio operator strains to hear orders from his platoon leader over the howling desert wind. Scouts peer out from a boulder-strewn hilltop, while TOW gunners nestle in the cracked bed of a desiccated river. Suddenly, an explosion of machine-gun fire pierces the pre-dawn silence; the clamor grows as the thunderous, baritone booms of tank guns commence.

To the staff at the Army's National Training Center (NTC) at Ft. Irwin, California, this frenzy of warlike activity is routine. To the 3,500 American soldiers out there fighting the "Soviet" menace, it feels like hell.

The NTC, which opened in 1981, for the first time allows commanders and soldiers to experience the reality of modern warfare without the cost of actual combat. General Joseph T. Palastra Jr., commander-in-chief of the U.S. Forces Command, calls it the Army's "premier training facility." What Steuben was to the Continental Army in the eighteenth century, the NTC is to the Army in the twentieth.

Currently 28 heavy battalions, including National Guard combat battalions, train annually on the NTC's 1,000-square-mile battlefield. These battalions fight an opposition force highly trained in Soviet tactics and equipment, while a computer keeps track of who is winning.

The resident opposition force has been trained to think and act like Soviet soldiers. Its job is to attack Soviet-style,

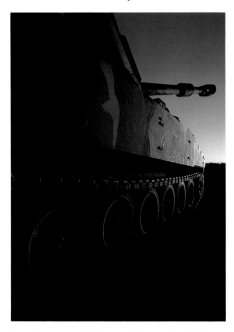

as tenaciously as possible, and it is probably better trained and prepared than the true enemy. "If you want to beat somebody in the Super Bowl, you try to find the very best team to scrimmage against," NTC Commander Brigadier General Pete Taylor explains. The principle of training by anticipating the strength and skill of potential enemies dates back to ancient Rome, whose warriors trained with shields and swords one-third heavier than those they used in actual battle.

Opposition soldiers are picked at random from throughout the U.S. Army for four-year assignments. Before they see action on the NTC battlefield, they receive intensive instruction at the Opposition Force Academy in a classroom whose walls are studded with images of Soviet weapons and tanks. They learn the Soviet military organization inside and out, and for several weeks they become Soviet scholars, studying the country's culture, history, and politics.

Most important, they map the psychological profile of the Soviet infantryman, whose indoctrination permits no deviation from the battle plan, even if it means death.

Opposition force soldiers receive an instructional book that diagrams dozens of Soviet infantry offensive tactics. They drill repeatedly, until the role of Soviet soldier becomes second nature. They also wear special uniforms—not a Soviet replica but one tailored in a Russian style—to set the "Soviet" team apart from the training battalions.

Most infantry attacks by opposition forces begin with heavy artillery fire that characterizes Soviet strategy. Chemical warfare is also frequently used by opposition forces on the NTC battlefield. Since Soviets are known to be prepared for offensive chemical warfare, U.S. soldiers must be prepared as well. At the NTC chemical-agent canisters containing tear gas, instead of paralyzing nerve gas and deadly hydrogen cyanide, are frequently fired by the opposition. A warning cry of "Gas! Gas! Gas!" is heard, and visiting soldiers quickly don protective gear. The gear reduces their vision, making weapons harder to operate, but learning to cope with chemical gear now rather than on a real battlefield will one day save lives.

Most mock battles with opposition forces occur at night. A sophisticated laser system is used instead of ammunition to figure out who wins. Each tank, personnel carrier, and soldier wears a sensor that records "hits" when struck by a laser beam. Soldiers are also equipped with starlight scopes and goggles that enable them to see through the night air, but the vast expanse of desert makes it hard to track enemy movement. At the end of the battle, the field is covered with casualties. Shrill noises identify "killed" soldiers, and flashing yellow lights mark "destroyed" vehicles. "That yellow light goes on and your heart drops right to your toes," a weary sergeant once remarked, relieved that his tank had been hit during a mock battle and not during a real war.

State-of-the-art computers provide a complete, detailed picture of the battle, based on recorded laser hits, that can be analyzed after the dust clears. Immediately following a battle, observer-controllers conduct reviews and diagram movements. At the end of two weeks of fighting NTC opposition forces, there is almost always a noticeable improvement in a battalion's effectiveness against the enemy. "The impact of making a mistake is driven home out here when the training soldiers see some 140 enemy vehicles coming at them," an experienced former NTC observer-controller has remarked.

The National Training Center is just one of four Army combat training centers. The Combat Maneuver Training Center at Hohenfels, West Germany, also specializes in heavy force training. Light force training takes place at the Joint Readiness Training Center at Little Rock Air Force Base in Ft. Chaffee, Arkansas, and the Battle Command Training Program at Ft. Leavenworth, Texas. NTC and other combat training centers exist because the rapid modernization of weapons has made early victories crucial to winning future wars. Douglas MacArthur once observed that "in no other profession are the penalties for employing untrained personnel so appalling or so irrevocable as in the military." Today's Army must be prepared the second trouble starts. The NTC and other combat training centers ensure that it will be.

It's a long way to the grueling challenge of a mock battle at the National Training Center. The road there starts with basic training—eight muscle-numbing weeks in which the Army does its damnedest to toughen up the flabby, speed up the sluggish, and drum out the weak. In today's Total Army, everybody goes through basic: officers and enlisted men from every branch of the Regular Army, the Army Reserves, and the Army National Guard.

To the uninitiated, basic training resembles a factory process where a kid is tossed into a hopper, a crank is turned, and later a trooper is spit out. But the process is much more involved.

Upon arriving at the post one morning, new recruits are greeted by a sign that says, "Welcome, We Train Professional Soldiers." Beneath those words, the sign painter should have added the Army's unofficial motto—"Hurry Up and Wait"—because that's what recruits will be doing a lot of for the next couple of days.

The first stop for recruits is the reception station, where a sergeant barks, "Show me your orders." From there recruits march to a barber's station, where the heads of male recruits are cropped close to their scalps; female recruits, shorn to above their collars.

At the next stop, recruits are issued a new wardrobe comprising combat boots and a battle dress uniform (BDU),

better known as fatigues. Gloves, shoes, socks, underwear, towels, and a duffel bag—all olive drab—are also provided.

Meals are served next at the mess hall. While training center food doesn't exactly merit four stars, it does offer a wide selection, from short-order items like tacos and hamburgers, to full-course meals, complete with dessert. "The best fed army in the world," Army brass like to boast.

During the remaining days at the reception battalion, recruits undergo a dental exam, inoculations, and mental testing; fill in life insurance forms and benefits paperwork; and receive their ID cards and dogtags. Once these preliminaries are completed, they buckle down to eight weeks of rigorous preparation.

WEEK 1 To recruits, the drill sergeant (DI) appears mean and tenacious. Under his Smoky Bear hat is a scowl

that he's been perfecting for 15 years. Most soldiers go through basic just once in a lifetime, but the DI will repeat basic a half-dozen times in a year. Recruited from the cream of noncommissioned officers, he considers it his personal mission to make the next eight weeks the most memorable, if not the most mind-numbing and muscle-wrenching, of a trainee's life. A short Army ditty sums it up best:

> When I get out of bed,
> There's a drill sergeant there.
> When I get out of bed,
> There's a drill sergeant there.
> Drill sergeant, drill sergeant,
> Everywhere I go.

There are numerous acronyms in the Army, but "PT," or physical training, is the drill sergeant's favorite. Recruits perform high jumps, squat thrusts, pushups, and other conditioning exercises at their DI's request, which may be several times a day. Whatever a DI requests, recruits always comply.

Recruits are taught the Army's way to clean the commons and the proper way to tuck blankets when they make up their beds. They learn how to wear their uniforms and about Army customs and traditions. By the end of the first week, they'll be able to identify a staff sergeant by his three chevrons floating over a rocker or a major by his gold oak leaf. And they learn to salute everything above them, even if it's "only a buzzard circling overhead."

WEEK 2 The second week of basic finds trainees continuing PT and other types of instruction, such as "D&C," drill and ceremonies. In addition they learn rifle-bayonet fighting, as well as undergo a wall-locker and field-equipment inspection.

WEEK 3 Pugil-stick sparring, land navigation, close-combat skills—these third-week experiences pale when compared to the gas-chamber exercise. Ten at a time, trainees wearing gas masks enter a chamber saturated with tear gas.

Once inside, they must remove their masks and state their names, ranks, and birth dates. The effects of the tear gas —burning noses and throats, aching chests and lungs— are immediate. When they emerge from the chamber, the lesson is learned: gas masks aren't an inconvenience; they're a necessity.

WEEK 4 By the fourth week, trainees begin learning how to use a variety of hand grenades. After practicing pitching dummy grenades, which explode but are harmless, from prone, kneeling, and standing positions, trainees advance to the real thing—fragmentation hand grenades. For this exercise, they move to the grenade range's "live bay" where they throw two live frag grenades apiece. From the control area, hole-ridden detonation pits can be seen behind a concrete wall. The first trainee steps toward the firing line, pulls the pin, hurls the grenade high and hard, and crouches.

Seconds later, a low, wide flash of light and heat announces the impending detonation. "I'll never forget the first time I heard that explosion," says a soldier. "The noise was horrendous."

WEEK 5 The main lesson of the fifth week is proper handling of an M-16 rifle. Trainees learn to align sights and hold their rifles steady. They also practice rapid fire and night fire and spend two days on a firing range. When it's all over, they must qualify at a minimum level of "marksman" by hitting at least 17 targets out of 40. To earn a "sharpshooter"

badge, trainees must score 24 out of 40; "expert" requires 28 out of 40. This week also includes individual tactical training, where trainees maneuver on their bellies under barbed wire, bayonet a dummy, spar with a pugil stick, sprint while live machine gun fire sprays above their heads, and climb over walls as simulated bombs explode nearby.

WEEK 6 An eight-mile hike faces trainees this week. They march in column formation, with staggered lines and five meters' distance between each trainee for safe dispersion. No talking or smoking is permitted. They are ordered to keep their weapons pointed out, because their enemy is not a fellow trainee.

WEEK 7 The final PT test takes place during week seven, but with six weeks of physical conditioning behind them, most recruits meet the challenge with little difficulty.

WEEK 8 While this is the last week, there's still much for trainees to do, starting with a tactical bivouac, where for several days, they dig foxholes, conduct bayonet practice, and scrimmage against other platoons. A 15-mile march back to post after the bivouac follows.

Only one more thing is required of trainees prior to graduation: the End-of-Cycle test, better known as the Super Bowl. To pass it, trainees must have mastered the wide range of material the drill sergeant has pumped into them for the past two months. Among other things, they must demonstrate their ability to administer first aid, set up and retrieve claymore mines, fire LAW rockets, and report to a commanding officer.

Upon passing the End-of-Cycle test, trainees have two days to take care of administrative business—turn in equipment and get files in order to take along to their next assignments. Finally, it's graduation day, when trainees officially become soldiers. The brigade marches onto the flag-bordered parade deck as friends and families proudly look on. When the pomp and circumstance is over, the new soldiers depart for the next post.

After basic, every soldier, whether officer or enlisted, regular Army or Reserves or Guard, receives training in a special field, better known as Advanced Individual Training, or AIT. A few AITs have been integrated with basic training —an infantryman, for example, completes basic and AIT at the same training center, for a total of 13 weeks.

Where soldiers go to receive advanced training depends on what military occupational specialty, or MOS, they pursue. An MOS is a soldier's official job description, and some soldiers acquire several MOS designations during their careers by taking advantage of various training opportunities. There are dozens of MOS designations in the Army, ranging from cook, to helicopter mechanic, to supply officer. Soldiers can train for a new MOS unrelated to their original one, attend special schools to upgrade an MOS they already have, or qualify for activities that fall outside of the MOS classification system, such as paratrooping. Below are profiles of three of the many different Army schools where soldiers can earn MOS classifications during their military careers.

COLLINS TRAINING CENTER, Fort Benning, Georgia. Almost new, the Collins Training Center is as sophisticated as the Bradley armored personnel carrier that it trains soldiers to operate. Millions of dollars worth of computers and simulators permit students to make mistakes without doing any damage, saving an enormous amount of wear and tear on the 25,000 tons of metal that constitute a Bradley.

The Collins Center has a couple of dozen "conduct of fire trainers," which give commanders and gunners an opportunity to experience simulated combat conditions that are very close to the real thing. Inside the trainers, the roaring engines and weapons fire seems so realistic that soldiers emerge battle-weary and drenched in sweat. The Hands-on Trainer, or HOT, assists in Bradley training by aiding master gunner students in absorbing the five-volume guide to trouble shooting Bradleys.

The Collins Center offers intensive hands-on training for all skills that are necessary to operate a Bradley at optimum capacity. A 10-day Basic Bradley Transition Course gives about 3,000 soldiers a year an overview of the armored carrier. Students of this course learn to fire the Bradley's weapons, drive through gullies, charge over ridges, navigate at night, and perfect mounted and dismounted tactics. Driving through pits of water and several inches of Georgia clay is often the trickiest task, since the Bradley can be finicky about water maneuvers. To qualify for the transition course, a soldier must already have an 11-Bravo, or infantryman, MOS. Upon completion, soldiers receive an 11-Mike MOS, shorthand for "fighting vehicle infantryman." As 11-Mikes, soldiers will be responsible for covering the Bradley's rear and flanks across the battlefield.

A four-week gunner's course qualifies 11-Mike soldiers to man guns in the turret, and a commander's course prepares staff sergeants through captains, who haven't had any Bradley training, for command positions with Bradley units. The most grueling course at the Collins Center is the 14-week master gunner course. Fewer than 300 attend, all hand-picked from the ranks of noncommissioned officers. By the time the noncoms complete the course, they will be experts at Bradley operations and training, enabling them to serve as a commander's right-hand man.

ARMY CHEMICAL SCHOOL, Fort McClellan, Alabama. Training soldiers to serve as chemical operations specialists, a 54-Bravo MOS, is the purpose of the Army Chemical School. As graduates of this school, soldiers will instruct and refresh their comrades on protection during chemical warfare. They also will be responsible for teaching soldiers how to use and care for their protective masks, suits, and chemical alarm sets. As well, they will teach critical wartime skills, such as contamination prevention and decontamination procedures, and give instructions in how to detect and identify various chemical agents. Although every soldier must be well-versed in nuclear, biological, and chemical warfare (NBC), 54-Bravos serve as experts when a crisis arises.

At the multimillion-dollar facility named after former chief Army chemical officer, Major General Egbert F. Bullene, soldiers practice detection and decontamination skills using tear gas and simulated chemical agents. But later, in training bays sealed off from the rest of the world, soldiers repeat earlier exercises using the real thing: nerve agents poured over vehicles and M-16 rifles that can cause nausea, cramps, convulsions, and untimely death. The stress arising from decontamination under real-life circumstances is much greater than when working with tear gas or simulated agents, and ultimately the lessons of the exercise will pay off. "I have no doubt that, once soldiers go through here—should they ever get called upon to use their NBC equipment for real—they'll know persistent from nonpersistent agents, contact times, little tricks of the trade," according to the chief of the decon training facility. "They will have faith in their skills and pass this faith on to others."

AIR ASSAULT SCHOOL, Ft. Campbell, Kentucky.

Started 15 years ago to standardize training for airmobile units, which often deploy from airborne choppers into difficult terrain, the Air Assault School offers a two-week, do-or-die course for soldiers looking for a challenge. Only about 65 percent of those who start the course will complete it.

Day one features a six-event obstacle course: the High Step Over (hurdles that must be traversed very carefully without use of the hands); the Confidence Climb (a tall ladder made of telephone poles); six vaults; the Low Crawl (muddy terrain that must be crossed in a prone position); the Tough One (a jungle gym of gigantic proportions); the Weaver (a pair of ladders forming an upside-down V, through which soldiers have to weave sideways), and the Gut Buster (a large perch from which soldiers perform a back flip and then, after landing, run a two-mile course while wearing water-soaked fatigues and jump boots).

Following the obstacle course, soldiers begin a three-part air assault training class. The first phase, combat air assault, involves mostly classroom training. Aspiring paratroopers learn to identify Hueys, Chinooks, and other aircraft types, as well as aircraft safety. Pathfinder operations come next, where soldiers receive instruction on setting up landing and pickup zones and guiding aircraft in. They also have to master 17 hand-and-arm signals used for directing helicopter pilots. Once soldiers pass the written test, they engage in a simulated combat air assault.

Phase two concentrates on slingloading operations. During this course, soldiers must absorb a wealth of highly technical information in three days if they want to pass. Slingloading cargo to a helicopter's belly is an exact science, and the tiniest error can result in the loss of the load, the aircraft, and the crew. Air-assault qualified soldiers have to be able to rig a load, and they have to be able to detect errors in loads that have already been rigged. Students are tested on the proper rigging of an A-22 bag, which holds up to 2,000 pounds and has a skip pad, two long straps, four flaps, eight sling straps, 12 side straps and buckles, a 114-inch chain, and a sling leg. To pass the rigging test, they must be able to identify four specific things wrong with the bundle—and they have to do it in two minutes. As many as 25 percent of the soldiers in the air assault school have been known to fail this difficult exam.

Rappelling techniques are taught in the third phase. First, soldiers begin by working on 12-foot inclined ramps to learn how to tie Swiss and Austrian "seats," body slings made from rope. When they rappel for the first time off a tower, with ropes secured to their waists and thighs, a belay person stands attentively below. The soldier on belay duty stands ready to stop the fall of any rappeller who plunges out of control. The luxury of having someone below to belay is shortlived, because the next exercise for students is rappelling out of a Huey helicopter 90 feet above the ground. After a mentally and physically grueling two weeks, the course ends, but not before soldiers complete an arduous 12-mile march.

The quiet beauty of Gothic buildings clustered on the Hudson Highlands is deceptively serene. It is Reception Day, better known as R-Day, and the newly arrived cadets are not coming to enjoy the scenery. They are an elite group—of more than 14,000 applicants to the Academy,

better known as West Point, only about 1,300 are accepted—but for the next year, these men and women will be bottom-of-the-totem-pole plebes. Dubbed by one newspaper as "America's choosiest college," West Point has earned a reputation for being a tough school. But students who stand up to the challenge will one day join a long and distinguished list of Academy alumni, including Ulysses S. Grant, George Armstrong Custer, John J. Pershing, George S. Patton, Douglas MacArthur, Omar Bradley, and Dwight D. Eisenhower.

While the Reserve Officer Training Corps (ROTC), found at various colleges and universities throughout the United States, and the Officer Candidate School at Fort Benning, Georgia, also are crucial for ensuring that the Army has a pool of well-trained leaders to draw from, the U.S. Military Academy at West Point possesses the longest history and deepest sense of tradition. A statue of General George Washington, who once established a Revolutionary war fortress where the academy now stands, presides over the parade field, where cadets will march in formation at the end of their very first day.

But first cadets are shorn and outfitted with new clothing and equipment. With as much dignity as possible, they begin their four-year term while wearing the mandatory white T-shirt, black shorts, black knee socks, and dress shoes required of all plebes. Upperclassmen teach the new cadets right away about the privileges of rank by ordering them to move faster, slow down, or tuck in their shirts. During their first year, cadets may only respond to questions in one of four ways: "Yes, sir (or ma'am);" "No, sir (or ma'am);" "No excuse, sir (or ma'am);" and "Sir (or ma'am), I do not understand." First-year cadets must salute all upperclassmen, and when passing through Washington Hall's tunnels, they must brush one shoulder against the wall.

Cadet basic training, six and a half weeks of hard work and mental exertion, is so rigorous and exacting that cadets cannot drop out of the Academy until they have completed four weeks of it. Those who remain will continue their education for four years, training for careers as officers of the Regular Army. After successfully completing classes ranging from military history and training to engineering and the humanities, cadets will earn their baccalaureate degrees. There are approximately 13,000 U.S. Military Academy graduates in the Army today.

(Above) Airborne training at Fort Benning, Georgia, is as democratic as the military gets. Anybody who possesses the rigorous physical and mental qualifications needed by parachutists has a chance to earn the coveted "silver wings" of an Army parachutist. (Overleaf, page 65) A drill sergeant, outfitted in "Smokey Bear" hat and battle-dress attire, stands beside a rappelling platform. His responsibility involves instructing soldiers in the life-or-death fundamentals of rappelling techniques.

Infantrymen were called "dog faces" during the world wars; the term probably derived from the unshaven look of soldiers in combat. Today "grunt" is the most common nickname used. Popularized during the Vietnam era, the term refers to a soldier's groaning strain when lifting heavy battle gear.

(**Above and facing**) Every soldier must face the rigors of basic training. "The first virtue in a soldier," French General Napoleon Bonaparte once said, "is endurance of fatigue."

(Above and facing) Basic training ranges from physical training to drill and formation instruction. The purpose of the eight-week basic training course is to turn raw recruits into battle-proficient soldiers capable of surviving on the modern battlefield.

The brutal reality of close combat is integral to Special Forces training.
These elite warriors must be able to operate in the most hostile envi-
ronments through reliance on their own disciplined expertise.

(Above) Special Forces soldiers even take their lockers seriously. President John F. Kennedy authorized the wearing of the green beret, designating it a symbol of excellence, a mark of distinction, and a badge of courage. **(Overleaf, pages 74-75)** Combat swimmers are part of the infiltration techniques used by Army Special Forces.

(Above) A soldier practices with a communist assault rifle during a Military Intelligence training program. Military Intelligence is one of the most crucial branches of the Army. **(Facing)** Soldiers receive instruction on all types of foreign, especially Soviet-bloc, weaponry.

(Above) A soldier fires a Stinger missile on a simulated training aid. The landscape is projected onto a surface that functions like a panoramic movie screen. (Facing) At night mechanized infantrymen are bathed in the harsh red glare of the infrared battle zone. Special goggles worn by soldiers permit them to see the infrared spectrum.

Intense low-level flight skills, demanded by the Army's Aviation branch, are stressed during helicopter training at Fort Rucker, Alabama.

(Above) Infantrymen learn standard air assault techniques by rappelling off a tower before being dropped on ropes from helicopters. Paratrooper trainees are harnessed to cables during their jump from the 34-foot tower as they practice proper procedures for exiting an in-flight aircraft.

(Above) The President of the United States is the commander in chief of the United States Army. Here President Reagan salutes cadets during a review at the U.S. Military Academy, West Point, New York. The Academy is currently one of the oldest military schools in the world. **(Facing)** A West Point cadet checks his uniform prior to a parade formation.

THE SOLDIER'S MISSION

The United States Army soldier is part of a highly technical military force dedicated to one mission: maintaining the country's national security in peace or war. Today's Army is highly diversified and sophisticated, with many units tailored for specific tasks. But each component is manned by soldiers who, as individuals, perform the vital roles that guarantee the nation's defense. A soldier's exact job will often depend on the type of unit being served, but many soldiering attributes are common to all Army personnel.

The Army's soldiers have to be highly trained and motivated because the Army must be ready at all times to perform a wide range of missions. These cover both current assignments, which are keyed to present political responsibilities and treaty obligations, and future global contingencies. In many cases the Army is the only service with the capability to get the job done. The importance of each individual soldier's effort is well understood by the leaders at the top. Army Chief of Staff General Carl E. Vuono stated, "The absolute number one priority for the Army is to attract and retain quality soldiers."

The foremost task of a soldier is to know how to fight and survive on the battlefield, while continuing to perform a selected task necessary to keep the team—whether it be a squad or battalion—in fighting trim. A soldier must be skilled in duty performance and have confidence in using the weapons and tools of war. The soldier's training really begins in earnest after completion of basic schooling, once the soldier is part of a unit, and continues at a relentless pace geared to sharpen acquired knowledge and team spirit.

In wartime the soldier's training will be put to the ultimate test—units rehearse their missions constantly in field and garrison. The battle drill is often tough and realistic, with emphasis placed on enduring hardship. Tomorrow's battlefield is expected to be a violent mix of fluid action. Situations may develop where mobility and the shock of combat will tear apart a cohesive front line, severing units from each other and sources of supply. The Army must

Soldiers based in South Korea prepare for maneuvers. The Army remains on duty in that country to assure the continued viability of the South Korean state following the war of 1950 to 1953.

continue to operate effectively in order to win; therefore, Army soldiers must be prepared to master the most difficult circumstances and still retain combat and technical proficiency.

The discipline of the soldier provides the basis for unit cohesion and battlefield success. A soldier's discipline and unit pride, or esprit de corps, provide the fundamental building blocks for mission accomplishment. Military conduct is reinforced by a complex and sometimes intangible fabric of established customs. These include the soldier's salute, honor to the flag, insignia, awards and decorations, reporting procedures, and courtesy toward one's officers and sergeants. Throughout the Army's history, these soldiering traits have produced an individual and group attitude that insures obedience to orders and the initiation of appropriate action in the absence of orders.

The soldier's hand salute is one of the foremost examples of military courtesy. This tradition is so old that we can only guess when and where it started. Some say it began with the oldest military organizations as a means of preventing personal assassinations. People who wanted to see important military officials had to come before them with their right hand raised to show that they did not hold a dagger or other weapon. Others say the salute originated with a warrior's gesture of raising his helmet visor to show recognition. The more fanciful stories include the knight's shielding of his eyes from the dazzling beauty of some high-born lady sitting in the jousting arena. Whatever its

mysterious past, saluting is now part of the respectful exchange of greetings between soldiers of different ranks.

The post of honor comprises another set of soldiering traditions. Junior soldiers always walk to the left of superiors, a custom commonly traced to the times when fighting was accomplished with swords and clubs. Because most warriors were right-handed, the superior soldier was accorded the honor of defending the right, and the junior soldier shielded the left side from attack. Sergeants and officers are still called to the front and center of parade formations, a practice derived from the days of marching armies, when officials were called forward to receive secret or last-minute instructions from their commanders.

The soldier's manner of reporting for duty, walking with an officer, riding in an official vehicle, and even speaking in a military setting are all geared toward producing discipline and prompt combat response. Many peacetime formalities are dropped in combat, where a radio operator's courtesy during transmission might belie a unit's hierarchical arrangement or a saluting-type gesture would expose a leader to mortal danger from enemy snipers. Whenever possible, however, the soldiering codes of conduct are strictly adhered to. When combat conditions permit, even the soldier's more pronounced courtesies are quickly reinstated.

The clothes of a soldier constitute the uniform. Uniforms are prescribed by international law and custom and are designed deliberately to distinguish soldiers from civilians. Uniforms also have practical applications, such as differentiating rank and enabling a soldier to work in comfort. The goal of military comfort is not comfort in the ordinary sense, but the avoidance of acute discomfort that impairs combat efficiency because of cold or heat conditions, thus limiting soldiering performance.

Formal uniforms are worn during duty that does not require hard physical labor and may be embellished with decorations and other recognitions of a soldier's accomplishments. These type of uniforms are designed primarily to enhance the soldier's appearance and morale. The method of wear and type of headgear or footwear may also differentiate between units within the Army.

The soldier's fatigues serve as a working uniform that can withstand more rugged use and become dirty without undue concern. These are often supplemented by apparel, such as overalls, that can be donned by mechanics or repair personnel. Specialized working uniforms are produced for decontamination personnel, vehicle crews, and aviators. The working uniform may also double as a duty uniform or a battle dress uniform.

The soldier's battle dress uniform is part of the fighting ensemble. It often includes camouflage clothing to hamper enemy marksmen or protective clothing needed to shield the soldier in a radioactive, chemical, or biological environment. The soldier also carries an assortment of combatant gear on the battle uniform. These accessories include the individual equipment harness and belt, ammunition cases, canteens, and other items needed close at hand.

Insignia is displayed on the soldier's uniform. The use of insignia to distinguish marks of authority or identification

predates recorded human history. Military insignia consists of metallic or cloth-embroidered articles worn on the uniform. These badges identify the wearer's rank, branch of Army assignment, duty capabilities, unit or organization

being served, and even the person's name. The soldier is expected to take excellent care of his uniform and insignia, and the professional soldier exhibits a great deal of pride in its correct wear.

The soldier's military courtesy and uniform maintenance reflects the quality of Army leadership. This leadership is entrusted to officers and sergeants, who are also soldiers. Their ability to command and enforce discipline, combined with the individual ability of each soldier, gives the Army its degree of integrity and ultimate mission capability.

Leadership is the primary function of all commissioned officers, and they are eligible by law to exercise command. They are appointed by the President of the United States and receive their authority from this appointment. Specialization at a particular skill is the primary function of all warrant officers. Warrant officers are appointed by the Department of the Army, and they derive their authority from this appointment. Officer and warrant officer rank insignia are metal pins in the shape of bars, leaves, eagles, and stars.

As an organized military force, the Army has bestowed its officers with many characteristics that can be traced to the most ancient human division of authority. Through time, the distinctions between higher leaders and the "common man" became legalized in a series of developments that eventually created a class of nobility in most societies. When the United States was liberated from its formal colonial status by the revolutionary army, the nobility was terminated within the new country. Many of the trappings of nobility, however, were retained for officers requiring a stern hand in the continental and frontier armies, and these have been carried down in modified form to the present day.

The relationship between enlisted and officer soldiers reflects this tradition, sometimes presenting a difficult scheme of proper behavior for democracy-minded Americans. This relationship is revised from its harsher aspects, but the fundamentals remain unchanged. The attitude of the enlisted soldier toward an officer is ideally mandated as one of respect, understanding, and helpfulness. The soldier is expected to obey an officer's orders and to show respect but is also encouraged to take problems to them and offer sound criticism if justified. Officers and other soldiers are taught to avoid overt social fraternization with their officers because familiarity often breeds disrespect and interferes with getting the job done.

Privates, specialists, and noncommissioned officers constitute the enlisted ranks. The noncommissioned officer serves as the actual soldiering backbone of the Army. While noncommissioned officers have the authority to give orders and have these orders obeyed, they differ from officers in that their authority is derived from Army regulations. Their authority is also earned, as a noncommissioned officer is given rank, or "stripes," in accordance with the demonstrated ability to lead others.

Army noncommissioned officers are the primary trainers and leaders of the mass of ordinary soldiers. They provide the basic care for the common soldier, including equipment and sustenance, direct most daily activities, and give the majority of instructions. The proximity of noncommissioned officers to their soldiers places them in the best position to pass along Army traditions and details of a given mission.

The sergeants, as noncommissioned officers, serve as the primary line supervisors and foxhole leaders in everyday work circumstances, drill, and time of war. Most maneuvering units at the fighting edge of the battlefront—fire teams, squads, and in many cases platoons—are led by sergeants. The sergeants are expected to function as officers if their leaders are killed or incapacitated in combat. There is good reason for the adage that the Army is only as good as its sergeants are capable.

In the old Army the crusty, veteran sergeant was sometimes obeyed more out of fear than respect. The noncommissioned officers of the "old days" could mete out any number of unpleasantries to back up their power, from withholding weekend passes to hours of grueling, dirty work in mess hall kitchens. Corporal punishment, although not sanctioned officially in many cases, was often dished out with regularity. This unchecked authority invariably led to abuses within the system as tyrannical sergeants became virtual czars within units led and staffed by weak or timid officers.

In today's Army, the noncommissioned officer has risen to a completely new height of professionalism. The sergeant's reliance on the soldier is based primarily on leadership and competence, because the soldier has been released from many of the petty duties that permitted nonjudicial punishment to exist. The entire process of a modern, professional noncommissioned officer corps actually started in the jungles and rice paddies of Southeast Asia, as brave soldiers were promoted in the field to replace heavy losses. These were generally well-educated, highly intelligent soldiers who possessed a keen sense of individual citizens' rights nurtured by the liberal tone of the era.

Unfortunately, the Vietnam-era noncommissioned officer has been unfairly blamed as being part of the unfounded "Army breakdown" in Vietnam. Many of these false charges have been sensationalized in a string of inaccurate, but highly praised, "realistic" war movies and repeated in scores of books and magazine articles. The Army did face severe personnel problems during its protracted conflict in Vietnam, but most of these can be traced to the numerical lack of noncommissioned officers, and certainly not to the ones who did serve. The Vietnam-era soldiers actually constituted some of our country's most proficient and loyal combatants, and they shaped the entire destiny and excellence of the present Army.

The soldier's home is the unit, whether it is situated in a row of barracks and office buildings or in the mud and snow of a field encampment. Properly informed soldiers are justly proud of their unit's past accomplishments, and these former wartime exploits add to the collective pride existing in every well-fed establishment. The long history of the U.S. Army has accumulated an abundance of rich heritage for these soldiering outfits. Where a civilian might see a senseless array of numerical entities, the soldier grasps the distinctive personality of each.

The 7th Infantry helped man the thin American lines in front of New Orleans during the War of 1812. To reinforce their position against the pending onslaught by Europe's best soldiers—British troops fresh from a victorious final campaign against Napoleon—the defenders heaped cotton bales in front of their lines. During the ensuing battle, the riflemen of the 7th Infantry decimated the British ranks. Today the regimental crest contains a banded cotton bale staked on two bayonets, and the regiment is still called the "Cottonbalers."

The 13th Infantry ("First at Vicksburg") features on its crest a Civil War cartridge box bearing the legend "Forty Rounds, U.S." During the height of that great war, the 13th Infantry was transferred from the Western Mississippi front to the fields of Eastern Virginia. Regiments engaged on the Eastern front usually wore the applicable corps badge on their caps, but the 13th Infantry soldiers unloading at the train station had no headgear emblems. A staff officer demanded to know the sign of the new unit. A battle-hardened sergeant loudly slapped his black McKeever cartridge box in response, roaring, "Forty Rounds, U.S.!" The fighting spirit of the 13th Infantry is still displayed by this symbol on its coat of arms.

During the fiercely opposed international relief expedition to Peking in the Chinese Boxer Rebellion of 1900, two companies of the 14th Infantry became pinned down by heavy fire between the towering abutments of the Chinese walled city. A gallant trumpeter volunteered to make the

perilous ascent of the fortified wall with the words, "I'll try, sir," and succeeded in raising a large American flag at the top. The regiment celebrates the Peking battle with an imperial Chinese dragon emblazoned on its crest, and is still known as the "Golden Dragons."

The 27th Infantry commemorates its courageous service in the Siberian American Expeditionary Force between the world wars with its own distinctive badge that bears a wolf's head above the motto, *Nec Aspera Terrant* ("Frightened by No Difficulties"). The howling winter wolves of Siberia are forever remembered by the regiment's proud title, "The Wolfhounds."

The leading elements of the 35th Infantry stormed Red Beach on Leyte Island in the Philippines during World War II, but they were temporarily stalled by heavy machine gun and rifle fire from Japanese pillboxes and bunkers. The regimental commander rose to his feet, rifle in hand, and waved his men forward, "Follow me!" The incident is graphically depicted by the infantryman's statue at the Army's Infantry School at Fort Benning, Georgia. The school's shoulder sleeve insignia contains the inscription *Follow Me* over a rifle bayonet design.

The above samples of valor are just a few examples from the Army's long muster roll of units and their soldiers. Today's successful soldiers intend to carry on these high standards established by Army tradition.

To accomplish the mission, the soldier must have pride, confidence, and a degree of self-determination in both challenging and routine tasks. Each should also enjoy a professional working relationship with supervisory personnel and must acquire the ability to endure and succeed under hostile conditions, regardless of the odds or obstacles of the enemy, weather, and terrain.

Noncommissioned and commissioned officers insure continuity of training and set the example for their soldiers. This ongoing training for waging war anticipates the hazards of battle and strives to improve individual skills, physical conditioning, and competitive spirit. The training must be rugged enough, within acceptable safety limits, to test the soldier's confidence and ability to overcome fears.

The soldier of the past was merely part of a rigid human killing machine designed to mow down enemy forces in set-piece battles and even cause terrorist paths of destruction to intimidate enemy resistance efforts. Little initiative was sought from dragooned ranks tuned to march to the sound of the drums and wade through volleys of fire. This process reached its most absurd impasse during the stalemated engagements of World War I. The advent of mechanized warfare in the following world war, along with succeeding breakthroughs in machine power, mobility, and human control, has brought tactical decision within the realm of the common soldier. In Vietnam numerous fire fights were decided by 20-man platoons and even six-man ranger patrols.

Today's soldiers, of course, perform a multitude of tasks that extend well beyond the old soldiering staples of foot infantry, cavalry, and horse-drawn artillery. Air defense artillery personnel scan the skies from ultra-modern command and control centers and man air-defense guns and missiles. Armor troopers are prepared to deploy their highly complex, mobile fighting machines in devastating attacks across the battlefield. Aviators and aviation-branch soldiers demonstrate their prowess on a continuous basis in hazardous flight and rescue missions.

The soldiers in the Corps of Engineers render construction and combat engineer services, as well as a host of other duties ranging from utilities maintenance to flood control. Field artillery personnel are familiar with a sophisticated range of heavy and lightweight artillery weapons, fire direction control apparatus, target acquisition systems, and both conventional and nuclear munitions. Infantry personnel give the Army its main fighting components, patrol rugged border regions, and provide most elements for prompt reaction missions throughout the world. Special Forces troopers are specialized in strategic reconnaissance, raiding, assisting foreign internal defense, and unconventional warfare.

Chemical Corps soldiers give the Army its expertise concerning all aspects of nuclear, biological, and chemical warfare, including field-flame expedients, smoke operations, and decontamination. The soldiers within Military Intelligence render support in intelligence and counter-intelligence activities and many other intelligence-related fields, such as electronic security and warfare. Military Police Corps soldiers secure the Army's rear areas and lines of communication, protect special weapons and com-

mand posts, and handle prisoners. Signal Corps soldiers maintain the vast tactical and strategic communications networks and systems on an Army- and Defense-wide basis.

The soldiers of the Adjutant General Corps provide technically advanced personnel services. Clergy and their enlisted assistants serving in the Army are part of the Chaplain Corps. Soldiers of the Finance Corps are responsible for pay operations and Army financial support. The personnel of the Judge Advocate General's Corps, humorously referred to as the "World's Largest Law Firm," administer the Uniformed Code of Military Justice and serve as a military law force. Ordnance soldiers maintain the Army's ordnance-type equipment, ranging from tank and automotive materiel to guided missiles. Quartermaster soldiers are responsible for the inventory and flow of general Army supplies. Transportation Corps soldiers are responsible for moving troops and cargo, by using every conceivable method from helicopters and trucks to barges and amphibian watercraft.

The personnel of the Army Medical Department serve in six main areas or "Corps." In addition to the general Medical Corps, these personnel may serve in the Dental Corps, the Nurse Corps, the Veterinary Corps, the Medical Service Corps, and the Medical Specialists Corps. Army soldiers in all medical fields are used to staff hospitals and medical facilities throughout the military.

Present and future soldiers of the Army are faced with a multitude of challenging opportunities. On the leading edge of technology, they must have a quick grasp of changing trends and an ability to learn completely new mechanisms and tactics. Robotistic devices and machines are taking over more and more of the soldier's monotonous and repetitious chores. Artificial intelligence-driven machines are being phased into the more demanding, dangerous jobs, such as reconnaissance expeditions and explosive demolition. In turn, soldiers are being counted upon to develop more flexible responses, handle more sophisticated equipment, and understand more interrelated processes.

The soldier's hallmark reflects the human dimension of war. Only the soldier can seize key objectives and hold them against counterattack on a permanent basis. As long as the human race insists on open conflict as the ultimate resolution of national and political will, soldiers will be called upon to serve and fight.

No one resents war more than the soldier who has to suffer through it and witness its horrors. Yet most soldiers can visualize the disaster that unprotected freedom would invite and are thus willing to make a personal commitment in safeguarding the well-being of the nation and its way of life.

The soldier of the United States Army is a capable, battle-ready but humanitarian citizen who stands ready to accomplish the mission and then—as in past wars—rebuild what has been destroyed, trying to restore what has been lost. Above all, the Army soldier continues to serve as this nation's primary guarantor of freedom and future prosperity.

(Above) American infantrymen maneuver across a training field in South Korea, where the U.S. maintains the 2d Infantry Division at full wartime readiness. (Overleaf, pages 92-93) Weapons poised at the ready, these fully-equipped combat soldiers prepare to repel a mock invasion (marked by smoke-producing vessels) off the shore of Honduras. The U.S. Army backs up national commitments to allied countries by dispatching battle-ready soldiers throughout the world.

(Above) A U.S. Army adviser instructs Honduran soldiers in the operation of an M-16, the primary weapon of the Army soldier. **(Overleaf, pages 96-97)** Infantrymen are tested in defensive positions during Gallant Eagle 1988, an emergency-deployment readiness exercise.

(**Above and facing**) Binoculars and special-training adaptor devices are part of the necessary paraphernalia required in modern computer-driven exercises fought out by real troops on the ground.

(Above) Military policemen, seen here in formation during an inspection of sidearms, are a highly versatile, multi-purpose force. In the Army their duties range from escorting convoys and guarding prisoners to fighting as regular infantry during emergencies. (Top facing) The "Killer" nickname in front of this field tent reflects the typical gallows humor of the ordinary soldier. (Bottom facing) Soldiers go over a few details prior to a patrol along Korea's DMZ (Demilitarized Zone). This potentially explosive area remains one of the most dangerous assignments for soldiers in the modern army and a place where they can expect to come under enemy fire.

(Above) Battlefield leadership is a tough, demanding task, and successful commanders rely on constant situation updates from their front-line soldiers. (Top and bottom facing) Soldiers participating in Gallant Eagle 1988 are treated to a rare hot meal from mermite cans brought to the field. The stacked boxes contain vacuum-packed, standard field rations known as MREs, or "Meals Ready to Eat." (Overleaf, pages 104-105) A scout jeep tests the depth of a ford in advance of the 1st Cavalry Division's heavy tanks.

(**Above**) Soldiers in protective gear train under simulated conditions of chemical-biological-radiological (CBR) warfare. (**Facing**) Individual camouflage is a necessary ingredient of a soldier's combat attire. The best camouflage often takes advantage of existing natural vegetation.

(Above and facing) The Army Rangers are commando soldiers specializing in raiding tactics and precision strikes against key enemy targets.

(Above and facing) Soldiers are taught to use a variety of means in crossing natural terrain obstacles. Some major rivers can be traversed by soldiers in small, portable rubber boats.

(Above and facing) Scaling and descending mountains are all part of a soldier's work in crossing rough terrain. **(Overleaf, pages 114-115)** Training for house-to-house fighting in urban warfare has gained special prominence for soldiers tackling terrorist targets.

(Above) The Blackhawk helicopter—powerful, fast, and reliable—does everything from delivering Howitzers to lifting troops out of a lake. (Facing) Amphibious infiltration is a specialty of the Rangers and Special Forces. (Overleaf, pages 118-119) Soldiers train in rugged, cold-weather areas within Alaska and high-altitude mountains of the American West.

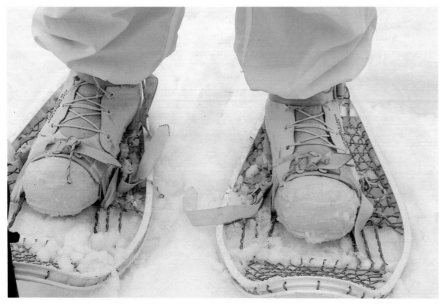

(Above and facing) Proficiency in Arctic-style warfare is expected of soldiers stationed in Alaska. These soldiers are equipped and trained for the rigors and climatic demands of a frozen war zone.

(**Above**) Ski troops are a necessary part of field units in the harsh Alaskan environment. (**Facing**) A Howitzer is cloaked by camouflage netting during support exercises at Fort Greeley, Alaska.

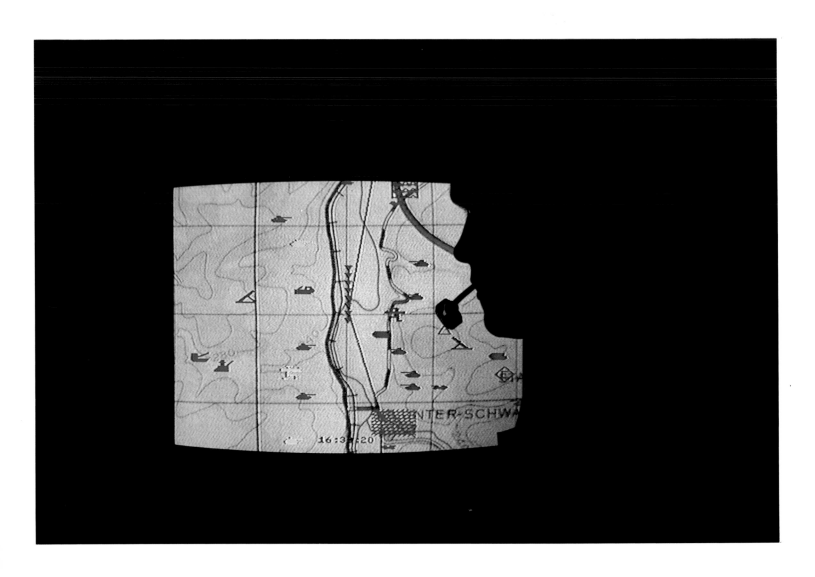

An Automated Visual Terrain Operator wearing communications headgear is silhouetted against the computerized graphic display of an un-
folding battle.

During training exercises, a computer screen reflects the progress of a war game as it gives instant data based on a wide selection of tactical options.

(Above) The key element of the Patriot missile system is a "phased-array radar." This sophisticated equipment can track hundreds of airborne objects simultaneously. It is responsible for surveillance as well as missile guidance. **(Facing)** As the satellite dish suggests, today's Army is increasingly dependent upon telecommunications systems. **(Overleaf, pages 128-129)** An older Hawk air defense missile guards a German field. Missile components give the soldier a sophisticated edge in discouraging enemy air attack.

(Above and facing) The Chapparel missile system is a mobile Army
air defense weapon that affords the soldier a degree of protection
against air attack.

A soldier prepares to fire a LAW (Light Antitank Weapon). This weapon provides the individual soldier with his own personal, shoulder-fired method for stopping armored vehicles or reducing fortified positions.

The trusted 90mm recoilless rifle is typical of an older family of proven weapons that are still present in the Army inventory.

The Vulcan air defense system is a modern version of the Gatling gun
and can blast targets with a hail of high-volume gunfire.

An Army National Guard crew loads a "Duster," a twin 40mm automatic antiaircraft gun on a tank chassis. The weapon has great lethality against both ground and air targets.

The Dragon, a medium-range antitank weapon, uses a disposal charge.
Such lightweight weapons allow the soldier to fight both armored vehicles
and reinforced bunkers.

The TOW (Tube-launched, Optically-tracked, Wire-guided) antitank weapon mounted on top of this vehicle can hit a target at great distances. Presently the TOW is one of the most widely used antitank missile systems in the world.

(Above) The mortar is one of the lightest, simplest, and best infantry weapons ever devised. **(Facing)** A lightweight field piece, the 105mm Howitzer gives direct artillery support to the infantryman.

(Above) A soldier sites a target with a Ground Vehicle Locating Device. His ability to detect and track targets is greatly enhanced by such modern apparatus. **(Facing)** Another soldier prepares to fire a portable Stinger missile launcher.

(Above) The "Redleg" soldiers' heavy and medium artillery provides the casualty-producing mainstay of war against enemy forces. (Facing) The MLRS, or "Multiple Launch Rocket System," can ripple-fire 2 to 12 rounds in one minute. This one is pictured ready to fire, but when being moved to a new site, the MLRS launch platform folds down into the bed of the vehicle.

(**Above and facing**) State-of-the-art war games are conducted at the National Training Center at Fort Irwin, California, where electronic sensing equipment keeps score on the battlefield and provides high-tech evaluation of combat units. The flash on the M1 tank at right indicates that the enemy has just scored a direct hit. (**Overleaf, pages 146-147**) An M1 tank firing during night exercises.

(Above and facing) The Abrams main battle tank gives the Army
a superb armored fighting vehicle for potential European combat. These
tanker soldiers racing to their crew positions form the armored backbone as the front line of NATO defense.

(Above and facing) Highly sophisticated and maneuverable, the Abrams main battle tank is an "iron dragon" without equal on the open battlefield.

(Above and facing) Armored soldiers stationed in Europe rehearse their contingency plans throughout both town and countryside in case of enemy invasion. **(Overleaf, pages 154-155)** An infantry squad deploys from its Bradley Infantry Fighting Vehicle. The squad can actually fire from within the tank's troop compartment using special rifle portals.

(Above and facing) An armored personnel carrier is a standard work-horse vehicle used for a wide variety of purposes, including mortar carrier, flame thrower, and armored cavalry assault vehicle. **(Overleaf, pages 158-159)** An M-60 tank, the Army's older, now-secondary battle tank, traverses the desert.

(Above and facing) An M-60 tank cruises a battlefield at night, using
its searchlight to spot enemy positions.

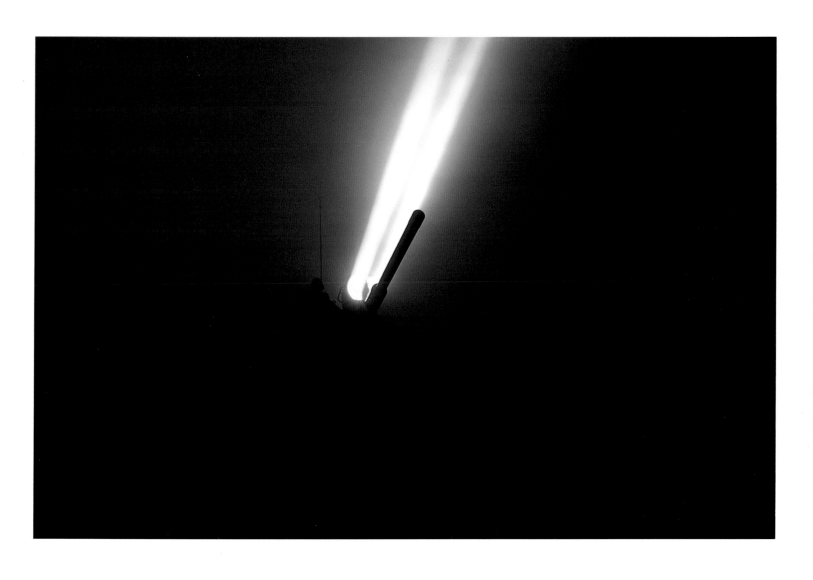

(Above and facing) The Army engineer soldier is equipped with a wide array of motorized construction vehicles. At right the Army transportation soldier keeps the battlefield supplied by using a mixed convoy of trucks and Hummer vehicles.

(Above and facing) The Chinook helicopter is an old but powerful helicopter capable of airlifting heavy cargo such as artillery or the fully loaded fuel bladders shown here. **(Overleaf, pages 166-167)** Chinook crewmen land in Honduras as part of an airmobile exercise.

A combination of airborne troops and Air Force transport aircraft give
the Army a quick-reaction, long-range strike capability.

(Above) The highly mobile 82d Airborne Division, "America's Guard of Honor," is prepared to deploy at a moment's notice throughout the world. **(Overleaf, pages 170-171)** Army airborne jumpmasters and their troopers rely on the skills of Air Force pilots, navigators, and load-masters to deliver them over targeted destinations.

(Above and facing) Pathfinders jump first to secure the Drop Zone and signal following aircraft to drop paratroopers in tactical situations. Descending paratroopers are temporarily vulnerable while traveling to earth under their canopies, but the restriction is negated once they are free of the chute.

(Above) The continual demanding field training endured by parachutist soldiers is reflected in the weariness of this trooper after several sleepless nights. **(Facing)** Aerial delivery can also take the form of rappelling, a technique used by most units in placing their soldiers on the ground.

(Above) A Blackhawk helicopter nestles into a tropical Landing Zone in Honduras. (Facing) Soldiers hustle artillery shells out of a Blackhawk in a timed training exercise.

(Above) An air-assault team rappels from a Blackhawk helicopter.
(Facing) Other soldiers are extracted on a "Jacob's Ladder" by a Chinook helicopter.

(Above and facing) The dependable, ubiquitous Huey helicopter can lift soldiers out of deep water or extract them from swampy terrain.

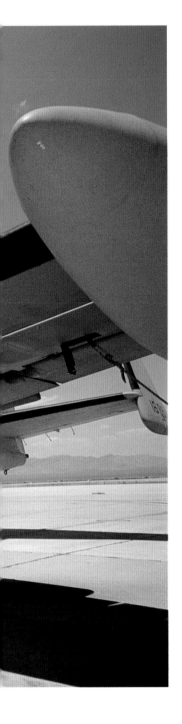

(Above and facing) In Mohawk reconnaissance planes, the pilot and observer are assisted by an infrared camera, which permanently records the terrain by developing a radar image on film. (Overleaf, pages 184-185) The Army's Aviation branch is dedicated to giving prompt and accurate aerial assistance to otherwise ground-bound units.

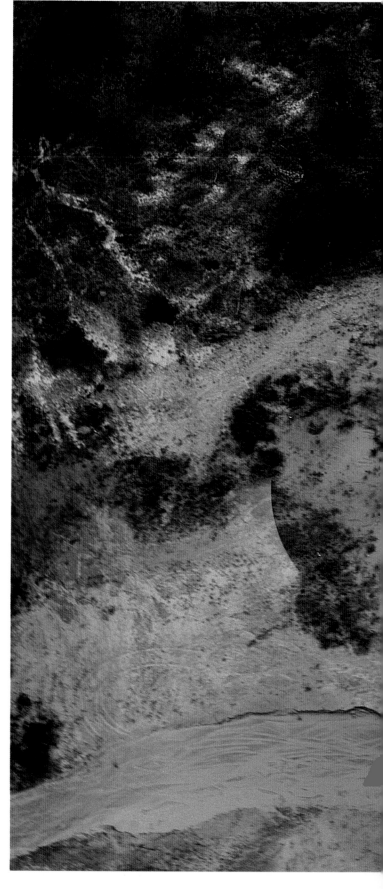

(Above and facing) The streamlined Cobra, seen facing and in the foreground above, is a highly armed attack helicopter that delivers its punch through rapid machine gun fire and missile volleys.

(**Above and facing**) In 1909 the U.S. War Department purchased its first aircraft, built by the Wright brothers. Today, the U.S. Army has a fleet of nearly 10,000 aircraft, including these helicopters parked on a landing zone and within a hangar.

(**Above and facing**) Apache attack helicopters provide aggressive close-air support. They guide their missiles with a sophisticated infrared laser tracking system. "That's one mean machine," observes an appreciative ground soldier.

(Above and facing) The Cobra's high-tech screen illuminates a target, which is then brought under direct fire from the helicopter's main armament.

(Above) Mechanics assemble a helicopter with the help of a crane truck. (Facing) Women in today's Army share many of the responsibilities of soldiering together with their male counterparts. Perhaps the most vital job performed by soldiers is the relatively unglamorous duty of mechanical maintenance.

A helicopter team hovers low to the ground as it prepares to seek targets
just over the tree line.

Army aviators are dedicated professionals who provide the ground soldier with swift on-call support despite the risk involved.

(Above and facing) Two of the main tasks of armed helicopters are surveillance and delivery of suppressive fire.

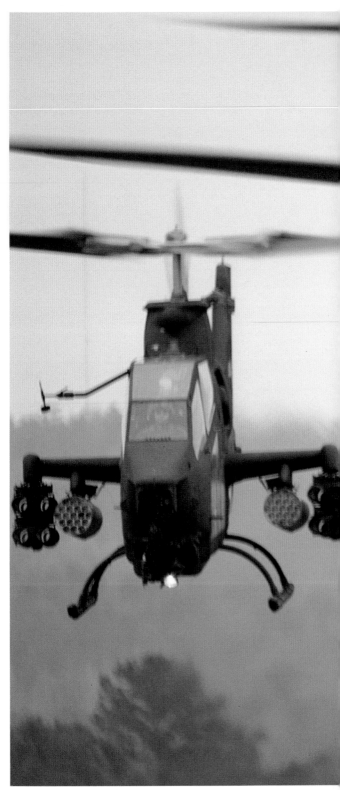

(**Above**) A band of sleek Cobras returns from a twilight mission. (**Facing**) A Cobra helicopter gunner checks his target sights. (**Overleaf, 202-203**) An Apache helicopter hovers over the woodlands, the normally expected terrain of any war fought in continental Europe.

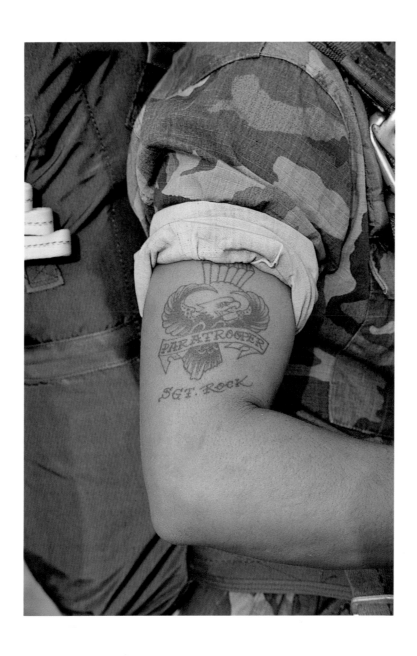

(Above) A paratrooper of the 82d Airborne Division. (Facing) A helicopter plucks a soldier from the sea during a closely coordinated extraction mission. (Overleaf, pages 206-207) Soldiers of the 3d Armored Cavalry Regiment.

The U.S. Army soldier stands ever vigilant as a sentinel of democracy.